—

10

4

2i

12 -

3. -

24. -

14.

4 Se

25 8

16/.

6/11

27 No

18 Dec

Luxe

AMY KEY was born in Dover and grew up in Kent and the North East. She now lives and works in London. She co-edits the online journal *Poems in Which*. Her pamphlet *Instead of Stars* was published by tall-lighthouse in 2009. Luxe is her first collection.

Luxe

by
AMY KEY

SALT

CROMER

PUBLISHED BY SALT PUBLISHING
12 Norwich Road, Cromer, Norfolk NR27 0AX

The right of Amy Key to be identified as the
author of this work has been asserted by her in accordance
with Section 77 of the Copyright, Designs and Patents Act 1988.

Salt Publishing 2013

Printed in the UK by Berforts Information Press

Typeset in Paperback 9 / 13

ISBN 978 1 907773 53 2 hardback

1 3 5 7 9 8 6 4 2

For Joseph, Elsie, Gene and Alexander

Contents

Acknowledgements

Some of these poems first appeared in *Annexe*, *Birdbook I: Towns, Gardens and Woodland* (Sidekick Books, 2009), *BODY, City State: New London Poetry* (Penned in the Margins, 2009), *Clinic II*, *Erotic Review*, *Instead of Stars* (tall-lighthouse, 2009), *Magma*, *Oxford Poetry*, *Penning Perfumes*, *Peony Moon*, *Pocket Spellbook* (Sidekick Books, 2010), *Poem Art Threat*, *The Quietus*, *Rising*, *Selected Poems* and *Smiths Knoll*.

'Brand New Lover' was commissioned by Holloway-Smith Noir to inspire lingerie design.

'Mother of Pearl' was commissioned by the artist Alex Carr.

'What of You And I' was commissioned by Writing East Midlands for the World Young Artists festival.

'Before The Waning Spiral Stairs' was commissioned by Penning Perfumes. It is a response to the perfume Encre Noir by Lalique.

'The Strange Message in the Parchment' was commissioned by Simon Barraclough, Isobel Dixon and Chris McCabe for the 'On a Trip to Cirrus Minor' event. It is in response to Pink Floyd's *A Saucerful of Secrets*.

'Spoilt Victorian Child' was commissioned by Stinky Bear Press for *Poem Art Threat*. It is a reorganisation of 'Spoilt Victorian Child' by The Fall.

I would like to thank John Stammers' erstwhile Saturday group and Roddy Lumsden's Wednesday group for their advice, but most importantly, their friendship.

To Lauren Laverne, Julia Bird and Claire Trévien – thank you
for giving me the most magic opportunities for poetry fear and
pleasure.

Heartfelt thanks to Wayne Holloway-Smith, Camellia Stafford,
Heather Phillipson, Claire Trévien, Emily Hasler, Sarah Crewe,
Nia Davies and Mark Waldron for your perception, sass and
encouragement. And to Roddy Lumsden – an ultra thank you.

To my family and those I think of as family – my love.

Poetry should be "uh huh" like ... "baby has to have it ..."
CHELSEY MINNIS, *Preface 1*

Brand New Lover

I've abandoned vanity, since I became a body
of pixels, never quite set, since you rippled
the apparent skin of me.

I'm all texture. Silk rosette, billowing coral,
tentative as a just baked cake. Sensations
slide over my knitted blood.

My mouth is a glass paperweight
to keep our tastes in, like maraschino
cherries and water from a zinc cup.

This is not about a future
with a decorative child. Layer your pulse
onto my pulse. Dress me.

Here, For Your Amusement

Colourwise I'm more meadow than hedgerow
though I have wooden clothes pegs and underneath it all
I'm comfortable as a smock. Less wild than a meadow.
I expect you will wonder what this is all about – well it's wrong,
like giving names to the eggs in the box.

Here is a picture of a horse very proud of itself.
Here is a drawing of a flower, from hundreds of years ago
– you will still find such flowers in the garden! There is
       something
you will want to understand in these pictures,
so you spend time with them. Perhaps that's what it's about.

I would like to be able to make a very nearly complete list,
of everything that matters to me, leaving nothing out.
Is that what it's like to be afraid to die? Also
to have the most inquisitive eyes and see beauty beauty
beauty pick away at the wallowing mortar.
To know the composure of a closed clam.

With You

For my sister

The fish gurgle in their outer space light –
I ask "pass me the blanket" and the wineglass
residues are violet and look back at us, like pupils.

To-do lists cascade from the fridge.
Your to-do lists are often niche catalogue orders.
We both eat showy pralines. Alternately, you eat
                    the lychees.

When you're distracted I like to hide my finger
in the core of your best ringlet. Upstairs the bath
lies empty and I can't but think bath oils and towelling.

I harvest garden moss and set it on the floorboards.
The garden is flung with a camouflage of twilights.
We turn the lights down and sit on the moss bed,

compare photos of our favourite light fittings.
If you do me a pedicure, I'll do you a manicure.
Your eating of the lychees suggests the extent

of your gentleness. My favourite: Hotel Kiev;
yours, in this living room. I choose to breathe
in the space between your breaths.

We've declined all other atmospheres:
the room turns aquarium. We sit back,
tune into deep-sea light shows.

Your eyes fill in with yet more green. Once
you sat by my bed until you knew I was dreaming.

Mother Of Pearl

a sky like rained-on whipped cream
      birth stones raked through a pond
palette of eye colours
      the swoop of a lavish bird at dusk

an aged mirror sky, all flatter and swoon
      pearl-cool lychees,
sugar-dusted jelly, icing the glitz
of a tipped-out button box

newly calcimined sky, clean
      as fresh almonds
spring bluebells – the polar ice

To A Clothes Rail

Dress folded as an envelope and posted to me
Hand-me-down dress taken up, then taken down again
The one worn once, to a party
Age-appropriate dress
Dress the colour of your skin long underwater
Margot dress, Marianne dress, Marie-Antionette dress
Paper dress, never worn, purely decorative
Dress employed as stand-in
Silk dress with scenes from Labyrinth
Pattern for a dress, unmade
Dress embroidered with every song I've ever loved
Pinafore that comes with caveats
Two sizes too small dress, bought for its primrose
One last seen doing the Hula down the precinct
Shift once worn in a dream
Dress as though assembled from vegetable peelings
Woodland dress in the style of a fawn
Poppy-print shirtwaist, won in a tombola
Dress for slow-dancing to 'Anyone Who Knows What Love Is
    (Will Understand)'
Fancy dress in want of a petticoat
Cocktail-drinking dress, un-sittable-down in
Dress best worn with brutalist pendant
Smock to bring to mind a meadow
Old-fashioned dress in crêpe with self-covered belt
Little black dresses (numerous)
Acid light projections dress for crazing the eyes
Formal wear gown for selling on eBay
Dress bought for funeral, frequently worn to detach from death
Dress last worn when someone cried for you

Fretful dress, to be cut up for rags
Palladium dress for looking into mirrors in
A cake of a dress – whipped to frou-frou
Scented dress of mustard seed, orange peel and almond milk
Glitter-bellied hummingbird dress
Ex-favourite dress, now not quite right
Perfectly acceptable dress, given the circumstances

Yes, She Seemed Demure

but I had seen her eyes flow over like a vase
beneath a left-on tap and how around her, the men's
patter stumbled like a high-heeled walk across cobbles.
No ordinary girl. I so keenly wanted to know her,
but she was unwearable to me – shiny harp-string hair,
the way her throat buttoned-up to mute – with my overt
everythings. One night I went home
to unfloozy myself, combed through my dresses
for shimmy and cling. Out went the showy. I shied
my tongue away from unbecoming talk, e.g. 'shrug'
and 'toothy'; studied my face into blank. Taking up smoking,
I swiftly acquired aloneness and never took a lover.
I remember once she winked as I glowered in a corner.
We saw her less and less that year.

Anthea In Paris

She wears a white dress
patterned with cherry sprigs.

Her afro hair straight now,
sleek under the red fez.

She casts off her flip-flops,
smiles, swings her legs;

her toenails gleam
opal – plunge into water:

dissolve the chevrons
of dust branding each cool foot.

Poem To A Year Lived In Camberwell Road

Times I felt caught under a cut-glass tumbler
– the light high and brittle – as when I was a child

and thought myself alone in the polished-wood
church, nervy and rapt. Other times, porous –

in the bathtub soaking up the citrine charge
of streetlamps. At night, my ambition

was road closures and all the nightlight sealed out.
The treacle-glazed floorboards invited contact.

When alone, I'd lie flat, my spine eking
itself flush to the ground. Often I was not alone,

but mainly I wiped down surfaces,
fetched the wine with ardent domesticity.

In the garden, blackbirds reliably tugged up
the worms; I burned the leaves.

Memories of that year's flowers gather:
celebration roses, daffodils almost sour,

an upset of lilies, delivered boxed-up like a Hoover.
Some I preserved, pressed like flesh in a surge.

Ornaments crowded the available surfaces.
Weekly, I added to their number,

as though I could borrow their delicacies,
dissolve the most drear of days.

Emotional State Seen Through A Pale-Haired Fringe

Dawn is coloured sweet pea and warbles with birds.
From bed, you notice how dust garlands

your fake yellow roses, but what now could
be gained by licking them clean? You could

plan menus, polish the mirrors, call your mother
and sweep the yard. Cleanliness, if not calm

in your reach. But, storm sultry, you lack
resources for comfort: the last velvet sleep;

legitimate wretchedness.
Others tell you, *I too have felt alone.*

Imagine them, teary on the sofa or wrenched
in the bathtub, all their wishes declined.

And then your own confines of lonesomeness,
where the at-boil kettle maddens the bully

of your memory, and no one there to see it blow.

Super Extra Gravity

kissing skirt unfurls in the alley • tender-stemmed
glassware dangled from tame fingers • a cinematic
gin bar brawl • your surrender to ultra texts • forgotten
green teas cool in the crush • the silver-brimmed
purse slinks out of sight • melt perfect spheres of ice
• cherry stalks idle in the bowl • every loaded thought
teased out • pale silk wears at the cuff • empty high
heels parade the stairs • twirl the heirloom parasol
• a stack of newspapers concertinas across the rug •
the feeling I'm a pebble beach you just walked across

On Typing Paper Stolen From Her Employers She Proceeds To Evolve A Campaign

A feeling that I should be writing a diary,
but every thought feels like an abomination. Like: drunk desire,
or cling-film bed sheets. My old diaries
bring on a feeling like feeling uncertain in someone's embrace.
How I lacked ingenious neuroses!
Meanwhile, I am in love with blondes
in the newest way passion can exert itself. But,
it was blondes who I first edged my knee towards,
some hours before intolerable kisses.
Lips I've kissed crumble like meringue.
Hopes should recede with age, but this isn't
a right-seeming present!
Mainly, I sat with the expectant feeling
of a passenger, for minutes and streets away
other things were possible. Sleep, a means of lace-edging days.
I could mock all my past's authentic woes
and the character I sketched out for a novel
that might be me: "23 years old, no imagination".
Surely I should be listening to other songs by now.
My imagined future is a collapsed soufflé.

You Talk Big, Young Man. Pray What Are These Riches You Speak Of?

It's a migraine wind   but I keep
the windows open   their invariant
thud   might keep an unruly mind
organised
       and you like my look
that's all   my body's ample
sufficiency   I encourage catastrophe
at each opportunity   I know this
about myself   and in respect
of your regard for me   you're right
I envy actors   their on-screen
debacles   and Saturday nights
give consent   to fret alone
TV conducting   my private face

Before The Waning Spiral Stairs

mouth whirled with steel-tinged rum • ale glazed the table-top •
slumped into acres of moss-damp hash • I saw the bleakly sequined
dawn • licked the tree bark's feline sap • resin drifted from a bow •
pushed you in the velveteen ditch • idly laced up in leather and weave
• sang 'Holy, Holy, Holy' • tended to wane mildewed pines • heard
cicadas burr as we sank to sleep • smoked my hair in a lime-washed
cellar • scratched lichen bruises from the bricks • bathed your heels
in the pewtering sink • kissed the remains • slaked the sulk

Luminaire

after Low at the Shepherd's Bush Empire

in the spotlight's vesper glare   I'm stripped
into exposure   my micro details blanked —
        lights   spin open their skirts
till my wax profile   stages a collapse
beneath shade   or I obstruct the dust
caught in the flukes of light   lit like prop
cigarettes twirled through   fat smoke
fingers of space outside the light   as note
against note   moulds   the air's bloom
sinks my skin   my ears thread in
the distinct tones   glide:
      as counterpoint   our lungs shift

Highlights In The History Of Concrete

Oh the very contrary sky is unlovely.

Dressed drear and billowing, she reflects
me sullen, with occasional polish and verve – she is not
there to compliment me.   But how I want her.

We would talk in Russian, and have synchronised
dreams of cosmonauts and gurgling pride.

Between us tents would be pitched on sand dunes
and all night she'd wail on the sea.   I pout
angles and slopes, after all, I want her to lie down on me.
To be her pavilion.

We Should Be Very Sorry
If There Was No Rain

For Sarah Crewe

I mention lately I've lacked a honeyed mood,
delicates have evaded me. Again I've spent too much
trying to ornamentally tile my life. The sofa's worn
down where I always sit and though my diary's
clogging up I don't know how to project.
I am ashamed to want a someone. Social
engagements are propelled by wine,
as unease goes up, eyeliner goes on. Sometimes
I imagine you in your kitchen, stirring soup.
Sometimes I make broth and pretend it will work.
Darling, it seems there's no awning
to shelter under. Or perhaps I'm under the awning
unable to step out. Someone might cake crumb
a path for me but it doesn't do to rely on others
to ice your day. I can see the dead roses
are as pretty as the live, appliqué
sleep to my brittle concerns. I have an aspiration
you will recognise my handwriting, in time.

Worn On The Body

I have seen plain black silk charged with your wearing,
you without it. Positioned you in appropriate surroundings
context being flourish at ankle or waist. I have teased
fabric away as it skirts bare skin, startled a slumped heart
with ribbon and bone. Draped a body in blossoms
of wool, comforting as oats.

And I have illuminated you
to prove the incongruity of a dress's atlas or georgette
to day or night. Dressed without reluctance
to herd my body into your parts. I have stood you
back to the sun, to disappear a pale shift. Found
how a dress can be a canopy for one bed or another.

The Susceptible Heart

Nothing to be done about the sky, its early fall.
You give me match-strike, candelabra, chandelier.
This year, autumn doesn't matter.
                              If lit by dawn,
my mind will clamour to recall how our kiss left off,
how the evening's talk – steeped in dramatics – set off
that wordless flourish. But tonight pours
into your absence. Take this half of ale,
sipped with one eye on your tastes and just now
my fringe swept away with your imagined hand.
Our romance, tracked by a fling of mill-town horns,
an elementary fiction of sweethearts.

Poem With Romantic Demise

He had a desperate radiance. We asked ourselves: what colour
would his lips be dead? We were somewhat nude in our wanting
for him. "When I am laid, am laid in earth" sang Mariette.
She'd mentally enclosed him in a tender glass coffin. I sought
out pyjamas I thought he'd like and washed them again
and again till the nub and weave waned. Me and Mariette
plaited each other's hair and glued seed pearls along our brows.
There were never enough cakes to go round. He'd once kissed
my wrist and this made me special. I cupped the kiss like a spider.
We wanted him dead, we were rehearsed for weeping. As he slept
we discussed how a death could be made. My tribute was long
prepared, and all the music chosen.

What Of You And I?

And dust isn't a medium! I place myself in a league of your friends, lovers and acquaintances based on appraised attractiveness. This vexes me. No, we have only this dust, prolonged domestic correspondence and snug jokes that will become someone else's. Well here are my scantily clad feelings, worn with regret. I've shown too much leg, but wine slackens my tongue. I have to believe there's a horizon over which my honesty is more tonic than liquor. What now for us? I have this dust to contend with, and more space to fill with your rollicking happiness. Even this crochet blanket won't address the lack of requited laundry. I have tinkered at sidekick, wifelet, fleeting fancy. I have worried over the paltry details of things that make up a person. I have let go, my tenderness without myself, see this heart on my face. And who could not but upset such precarious attachment? We were never in this together. I too have gathered dust under someone's gaze and will recalibrate all feeling. I stare hard at my inbox; switch on, off. We will end up friends.

Dearest,

I couldn't bear all the angles you could see me from, see? I'll take the blame for the mess I've made of rejection. I'd procrastinate about which knife to use to butter my toast. Where was I? I was forever shifting my chin, skirting the warmth of your cup of tea, the worn-down pile of the chaise. Forgive me? We can split the heirloom baubles – Harriet found me "over-worked" – and take the brown sugar lumps, my tiny silver tongs too. I like the idea of being where you are, still. I've adopted a new mode of speech, I now eat my crusts, but – I've fallen out of writing longhand, and with no longer a piano to play! I know you love them, these desiccating postcards. They seem too fragile to move.

Her

I think of her starlet lit,
of her mouth, sealed by peach skin. Of her preserved
in glue, her patent red hair, the faux fruit of her.
I think of her dialling a number
with a pencil – the phone being old – but I cannot
get the sequence right. I think of her besieged
by pigeons. Also I denounce the town crier, sudden
pigeons and the ATM. I replace her hair
with bullion fringe, and rainbow-stripe her eyes.
I think: yes, her boyfriend has died and I have his letters.
Of her taking a walk, the little bones of her feet.
I replace her with a Lucite statue filled with buds and illustrated
women of the '20s. I think of making loud noises
so she might notice me. Of her gruel-faced,
her pillow marked with black grit
like a cheap shoe in the rain.

Friend Vs.

Well he rubbed up against you the right way, it was correspondence –
but really, that boy was a chain of fairy lights to throttle yourself with.
Whittle down to the truth now –

Babe, this was *always* going to happen.

Don't let him reduce you to a pip-squeak, he's not worth
those mouse-pink eyes –

Listen Lovely, we *all* make mistakes.

And Sweetheart, he was never a suitable suitor! Let's plan nice
things to do, I have tickets for rooftop mini-golf and immaculate
martinis make amends for all kinds of things.

Darling, you *mustn't*:

Okay, in your own time, but don't you think you have a talent
for the catastrophic dalliance?! A bullying intuition must be paid
attention to. There's a pattern here. Let's paint your nails.

But A Love Poem Will Not Fail

After Chelsey Minnis

He made me cry like a girl denied pink bunting
Left my crockery lustrous with butter
Watched my school-flirt cartwheels
Ate the heads of nasturtiums
Let his doggy off the leash
Sang bawdy at the cream tea
Pushed me over in the daisies
Mistook my toenails for diamantes
Stuck his tongue into the Swiss cheese
Put his linen in the chiller
Knotted the leash to my ankle
Wrote I'm sorry in white petals
Poured cheap brandy on the bite marks
Had a thing for leatherette
Rubbed against the hydrant
Allowed the dog to chew the leash
Cheerled dances in the bathtub
Shot the Pepsi off the ledge
He liked me to wear the gold anklet
Milked it for all he was worth

Fortune Told From New York City

We sneeze out city filaments; apply lip-gloss in mirrored
cherries; down a chocolate-milk cuplet. Coffeed:

watch ornamental dogs parade shop windows;
allow our shadows to sneak into the day's captures;

try clam pie, pancakes, Peekytoe crab, Vodka Martinis
straight up with a twist. Shall we hitch up our skirts,

as in this city, it's all about the legs? At dinner,
when Rebecca tells me the wasabi has erected her nipples,

I drop my glass. Its waist gives way, brim slides to base,
Sancerre spools neat in my lap. We gurgle

out of Blue Ribbon wine-proofed to the storm: showers
aren't hostile after midnight. Street lamps know

how the sidewalk dresses in antique colours. The tales
I'm told have the insight of dust, older than I'll ever be.

His Is A Mystery Of Cooling Towers

demolitions and algae.
Oh suitor, thunder me
your elegant curse. Mobbed,
I will magic us to Siberian igloos
where lamps bleed a glow
into our symmetrical clinch.
Or a late shadowed terrace –
cool tumbles of liquor, a hand-painted parasol –
balmy with glossed austerity.
And though I will admit I was a squeeze
more drunk than you (given my rabble
of stunted views), I hold dear these inventions;
last night, after the third time
I noted my wine glass wanting, leaning close
and whispering my cheek
with mushroom-gill lashes, you murmured,
You, are a very nice girl.

The Strange Message
In The Parchment

Remember a day   before today
                        when the wooden lady sang –

her scarlet hands   and the view
that vanished   as the stars rose

its mystery sealed   in a tar-bound
trunk   and you couldn't remember

what the sound   of tapping heels
could mean   or whose locket was lost

at the crumbling wall   but then
those clues disguised   in the seesaw's

haul   or glockenspiel struck
at the crux   of the sun

Poem In Which

I describe 'tulle' and 'chiffon'.
His eyes replace mine.
In which I walk down Lower Marsh with a paper bag of apples.
The wind laps at my ankles.
I covet the turquoise paisley dress.
I relent – as you wish, as you wish.
I leave my flat to the sockless beatnik.
Poem in which I have sequined ears.
In which I visit The Empire of Tiny Dogs.
Poem with peeptoes.
In which there are marrowless bones.
I chuck out all my undergarments.
Poem scented with galaxolide.
I graze my memories with old photographs.
In which I have insatiable thirst.
Poem about pyjamas.
In which a man walks down Walworth Road in the rain, holding two
    battered sausages (unwrapped).
Poem written on the joy/doom axis.
Love poem to a chandelier.
In which again your actions are foolish.
Poem to conceal some feelings in.
Where I drink champagne from a coal-lined thimble.
Poem to avalanche in your heart.

Whoever You Are You Start Off A Stranger

till we edge beyond the fuzziness of presumed
contact.   Oh stranger boy,
your face is like mine. But we sign cheques with different hands.
Now we wear each other's cologne,
we have a cologne. The tendrils of our lungs
function harder when apart.
If you see this scarf around my neck it means
unravel the scarf from around my neck.
If you see this blanket at my shoulders it means
drape yourself about my shoulders. This is a dance
of not having to ask for things. Our limbs
are in sumptuous complicity.
We've become free of hoping to be beautiful
in photographs. Between us – it's a cinch,
and breakfast is always taken lazily. Oddball talk
will enchant me, endlessly, so tell those stories
as though we'd not yet met.

Valentine

Instead of I love you here's you: all cordial, necktie, vinyl
and cola cubes – the unsubtle quirks that make my heart wheel.
I'm the champagne in the saucer, you're the bubbles spun
by soap. No legacy of teacups can hold what I feel.

With you, morning hatches silly, buttery and plump;
lean to me, sing *belly, curve, loosen*. My platelets coo.
How the flex of your voice lolls in this devout climate
of sheets! Here's the nineteenth kiss in the queue.

Scott And Zelda

summer   retreated too young
slumped hips   her necessity of nerves
brutal pigments faded

pitiful dusty daughter
her inquisitive skirt   relic tiara
two step girl   wallowing under parasols

her evening dress   a gesture over skin
of pearls   modesty   lovely breath
vague companions   sucked in

the shore rose like something from home
      boys a distant image

[THOSE GIRLS]

reluctantly luminous   peculiar youth
frills pursuing   necks   ankles

girls clung   to rose   inkwell
to a mournful quilt   shared

paintless lips   no one fell on
gestures hatched   horizons sagged

beautiful cooed   the skeleton
wants   a nocturnal carnival

[IN THE SQUARE, AS THEY CAME OUT]

stern darlings   desire viewed from outside –
    mutual psychiatric
         conviction   love   and asthma
hope carried differently   intrusion glazed

oh he might!
                 correctness possessed
no suspicion   cold since Cali-FOR-nia

melancholy chemises   marble everything
         impatient as a dancer
                 a something gesture
submerged   early death swayed

[THE HIGH PARABOLAS OF SCHUMANN FELL THROUGH]

muscular sulks   imitating a girl
            twirled in a smoked glass atomizer
morphine ballet   precise toes   the hips of Midinettes

gloom announced the skylight   pudgy hydrangeas wilted
safety-pins   bonbons   pleated skirt
    the body's radiance aloof   obscurely skeleton

muscles – precise velvet
eyes filtrations   of iris   apricot   copperwire
    summon a lullaby   negligent fortune

Transmitting The Fatigue Of The Painter

After Wayne Holloway-Smith

you wore a cotton dress   over the cotton dress
    they scolded you for running into the sea
a dress cannot save you   no whitened thigh
broderie anglaised knees   rounded like doilies
    no dress   will make   a dolly of you
still wear the cotton over   cotton over cotton
till a princess gown   sags at your shins
    and your self-regarding hair
self-pout of admiration   they will scold you
for trampled hems   for you are both pout and scold
this is no picnic smiling afternoon   your petticoated ego
sustained only by petticoats   you should not run into the sea

Spoilt Victorian Child

past the trees, fairies	spoilt sugarcake
past the stairs, servant	smocked in grey
past the butterfly shrug	(fearful babes)
past tiger-cheek	disfigured with rouge
past green trees	toxic cakes
past the aqueduct	iced with pox
past stairs of books	avoid the mirror
past the reflection	the child

Igloo (Where the Wild Things Are)

When it is cold enough to slice the snow
we'll build an igloo and we will live in it.
The igloo will be like a poached egg,
the snow dome hiding a hot yolk. We will grow

sharper teeth and bedtimes will be later.
I will be cook and you will make fire.
I have stolen sausages from mum
and this will do us for tea. There is a story

I can tell at night of a runaway child
and you will ask if it's you. We have
two brothers, but they never let us take charge.
No one will know we are in the igloo,

but we'll find a way of telling we're safe.
Your best friend will be a bird and mine
will be a deer. The bird will bring us berries
and the deer will guard the door. Instead of talk,

we will have stronger thoughts. Our skin
will morph into something more warm. In summer,
we'll make bricks of mud to dry in the sun.

To A Runaway Child

From the sleep of the glade
sunburn will begin to tell,

at a felled tree's bridge
among the bluebell sprawl.

Escaped light evolves leaf
cells, exposes hides, buds,

irregular breeds; swallows
skate a few miles south;

an apple, caught in the river's
rip, gently bobs. Elements

correspond: this plant's essence
soothes skin puckered

by the flare, wild leaves make
for food. Curl up in the crib

of mossy limbs. Fall to the blur,
– a fascinator of blue.

Almost Everyone Who Has Ever Lived Loved Flowers

i.m. Eva Key

She lay back on the lounger to tame ladybirds
onto her fingers laced with the day's first smoke.
Lemon slices tipped from her G-and-Ts piled up

at daffodils' feet; while you stood in the beach sand
patch where nothing grew, catching a salty swell
in your throat, her cyclamen lips drew hard against the blue.

Pretty Please

In the yard there's waning snow
like clabbered milk, but mentally
I'm in an August-bleached field
and you have threshed a stalk of grain
for me to drink my cider through.
We identify as summer people.

There each lowered tone lifts,
burs caught on our socks are the sand
walked home from the beach. A suite
of songs sing California.

At night I prefer you lax – on, not under,
a blanket. When it's still warm, though the sky's
eye shadow caught in a crease, season
the rum with honey and lime and just let me be
your childhood crush. I want to not know
what to do; whether a kiss is on too high a shelf.

Caramel Swirl

Mine is the caramel with salt, a skirt and a tinselled belly.
It swirls like my swishy hem. Makes me maudlin
like sea frets, like sweetness – a buttery throat.

I need something to do with my hands.

Take me with my caramels and swoon
with sweetheart films where the beauty eats
bon-bons from a satin box.

There is nothing worse than pouring my own bath.

I need something to do – caramel-glaze the silver,
spoon praline from a crystal bowl. Ruin myself.
There is nothing worse than darning my own slippers.

I need something to get my teeth into.

Flirtatious State Seen Through A Hangover

The cherries were to be eaten in a cornfield at dusk.
I plump up the pillows and wallow with tonics,
waste days tongue-tying stalks into knots.
He is gymkhana, rosette and novel, but what can he give
save for daydream and stutter? He may dally sweet
in my eyes, but I know in my lips he could not dare
to kiss me.
           Wanting feels like too little caviar
for breakfast. I court delusion with inventions
of frisson, e.g. late-night, suggestive, elaborate emails.
Inventive delusion of knee-shifts and come-on,
meet restorative water, go home now by taxi.
Resist the urge to foresee your first child. Even
when his eyes check, in your eyes, his reflection.

But We Can't Marry Each Other

who'd pick up the bills? And people would look at us
and think: cousins? But I am thankful that it's OK to use you as prop
and aren't you just a packet of Ras El Hanout? Makes everything
taste better. I didn't like the idea of you with someone
but I saw you together and nothing quickened. You have to test these things,
the heart can be both prissy and pudgy. Apparently not looking for it
makes all the difference. I don't need to say these things,
I'm quite desperately readable, isn't that decadent of me!
We're ok, like pockets sewn up.
I sleep better at night knowing you would though.
Knowing someone would.

Poem With Hearts

heart cinched in
       left out in the rain
             bloated heart pumped full of drugs
heart written longhand in a letter
       potential heart
   my heart   your heart   dear heart
         heart in top hat and tails
cranky cold sentimental heart   orphaned heart
high maintenance heart   heart congested with 'you'
      pressed between blotting paper heart
you you you   paltry heart   heart of a coward
  heart you once knew   heart my mother warned me about
heart kept by another
      heart beset by falling trees

Au Revoir Baby

As, just for now, I want you flippant
as cocktails, and I want to drink the lot,
with a schooldays length summer
to come. For now I want Polaroid
dawns, sand in the sheets, gawky
handling of personal administration.
I'll be needlessly late, sense deprived,
forget all the messages.
The swag of what I may have in my eyes
and an aquarium-coloured bathtub
to paddle in. I want you presently, with no dither
of what now. I just want you present.

High Voltage

Just as I woke, you stomped into my head
and I thought of everything that makes me admire you:
not just your sass and nerve (although
it does deserve an explicit mention), but how
Neverland it is to spend time with you, like a pop-up theme park –
each day abundant with vivid wants,

like how you're era-less, confident as a portrait,
inconsolably hungry, you talk easy as an adult –
seems even your glamour isn't at the top of my list,
admiration being such an intimate reckoning of a

friend. If I can't say it now, when?
Oh, there's nothing ordinary about decadent warmth
real as foxgloves and glow sticks and winter birds,
did I tell you how much I want you to dance with me?

The Girl Other Girls Look At To See
What London Has Copied From Paris

Look at this girl with Hans Christian Andersen eyes,
audacious as jacuzzis. She's
undone in the way of a girl pictured waltzing
right as a calamity of rain swoons to turn
etceteras to ever-after.
Never without a rah-rah swish.

Look, here's a mother in David Lynch-blue
ankle boots so impeccably
velvet they deserve their own soundtrack. Her
evenings are bannisters to glide down,
revered and rescued by champagne or milk.
Now morning, the needle's saved from the run-out groove.
Espresso, toast, pharmaceuticals. Just listen to her.

Birds That Sing At Night

Then kiss me. Where's the accomplishment of waiting? (Tedious
hope keeps its own silly habits.) Kiss free from the indulgent
evening, glossy and afloat with nightjars and corncrakes. For the
ordinary. Scuzzy chemist, newsagent, revolving doorway, mistake!
Relate oh your clever feet, the pearl whites of your eyes,
extravagantly buttoned up blouse, things on toast.
Talk me through your lists. Let me in-to my own magic!
I want a saturation of sweetness capable of making this
crisis of a city bus open up like a gypsy caravan,
and you boy, a youngling in the Peacock Revolution, tonic suited,
lashes of a fawn, just someone sat opposite, ultra aware I'm here.

Going home I have you in my pocket. I have you in the boxsets,
in the playlists (indecent at the sink), the receipts. Today I wear a gingham
ribbon in my hair, just so. Undo me when my balance is lost.
Lino has never felt so good.

The Trap Laid For The Glittering Life

Coquelicot! That's how I'd describe your hair,
like how I'd imagine a cosmocrat's to look –
absolute pigment, primed for plumes and space minerals.
I love how I can always locate you in a vociferous
room and that you're more costume than wardrobe. Not
everyone can be as you are, and that's as well as a tucked in sheet.

Tell me I'm buttoned up the right way. That we will never not
reason it's okay to fall asleep on a stranger's shoulder before the projection
ends and we're blinked into being. We both know what's more
virtue than obligation and there's always a stash of gin
in the teapot because at times the obligations necessitate
endurance. Not once, but three times I have thought to call you at
night. Check I am still the way I am, and need not be.

Spell For A Sulking Room

Drab, low as an underskirt mood • limescale-dull water
glass • laundry pile tipped inside-out • wasted spray
of drooping ferns • moth wings palmed on the wall
• wine unravelled storytell • evaporate a quiet face •
deliriums of discontent • wring out the shabby lungs
• chide the tick of a parlour clock • amethyst-eyed
in your swooning • remember when this was about to happen

Interiorana

Ornaments spy on my quilt, its down
frayed where toes catch the tender

edge. The window rattles discontent.
Outside many tongues are flush

against their roofs, seeking an iced unison.
And in this room: flowers go to paper

as they sink down their measure;
an origami of ideas; socks steam

gently under the window; the draught
alerts my skin. To court day

I taste mineral-lush condensation,
unfrost the view, scent the room

with butter-sweetened pastries.
Over years, I'll acquire a chandelier

of silver spoons – each a different size –
some pewtered with age. When cold comes

they'll shiver high, bright tones.
Inside I fritter soft as cinders.

I Haven't Had A Dream
In A Long Time

Again I'm awake in a room full of dark, like cola
gone flat, thinking of those bodies, parallel to mine,

lying in their own attic rooms and the plump pigeons
roosting. To have always wanted an attic.

Today, the pavement webbed my sandals to the ground
with a feeling like candyfloss stuck to fingers.

Then there was the dirt, huddled in each fold
of my feet. I bathed them in the salad bowl, before bed,

and sliced cucumber for my eyes.
I don't understand it's too hot to eat.

The sound of police at this hour makes me say
'constabulary' out loud to disprove my suspicion

I may have forgotten how. Tomorrow, for tea,
something gagged with salt; freshly picked peas.

A nightingale flutes. It seems I do sleep.

Carry On Don't Lose Your Head

You, my doodling dandy, unfrock
the girls I know. I know
the temptation of bosoms,

the squidge of the bar
where girls come in contact
with boys and the prize

– a superb tremble
against the skin of another.
In this play of kinky heat,

some might wilt too soon.
Lace coverlets resign
to chair backs, cravats

loosen from necks.
Not you, my rampant boy,
heads are lost over you.

Fox's Eye

Only take away the very dead, mouldering
the air. Keep those that shiver cracker-dry,
their throats ceramic and petals pearl.
Let them loom more softly against the wall.
As everything in this room has gone brittle:
the pipes knuckle-crack equations, flakes trim
the skirting, butterflies fidget off mantles of dust.
In my mother's room, there was a fox's eye,
billowing and caramel, knotted in the wood.
To eclipse this scene, I will its gaze to me.

Pixellated

Still brittle from whisky   we start out with our ears
cocked to bird song   with a tight-throated skip
and perhaps   their beaks clip   poisonous berries
     to drop   in our gaping mouths
when we try to catch snow   as water apparently helps
     and though you feel dire   your blithe mood bobs up
till there's pink sequins studding the sky
     and winter's in pieces   kaleidoscope parts

I begin to turn   for the worse   the trees turn
creepy at the edges   and I quease at the toothy
dark gaps   and the bleach light
                              if you were to bound
     down the slope sloshing with laughter
I'd grab at branches   avoid the thorns
     and that abandoned glove   the sultry hand
of frozen wool   picked out in the ditch   braced with murder

Luxe

Snap your chopsticks cleanly.
In your curdling belly, keep down what the thighs
eek for. Substitutes include mink-lined dreams, wafers
of quince or rose. Substitutes are a drowsy let-down,
lacking texture, like an over-pouffed dessert.

Lavish yourself. Make eyes at yourself in train windows.
Think: this is an excellent posture for a girl in bed. Let your throat
turn in on itself with –
        your hands are raw with the putting on and taking off
of unsuitable bracelets. Want articulates like a chinking watch strap.
What you want to meet in you. The sunrise raw, sumptuous
canopies. To be the only person in the room.

Tight Dress

I'm in the tight dress. The one that prevents dignified sitting.
The tight dress suggests I'm prepared to be undressed.
Do my thighs flash through the seams?
I try to remember if the bed is made, or unmade.
The wind is wrapping up the sound of our kissing.
I wonder should I undress first or should you undress first.
I'm not sure I can take off the dress in a way that looks good.
I consider if I should save up sex until morning.
We are far gone and I'm better at kissing when sober.
I find that your earlobes provide the current fascination.
On my bedside table are three glasses of water and my favourite love letter.
I try to untie your shoes in a way that is appalling.

Some Day We Must Come Back
And Explore Properly

Inspired by a Russian matchbox from 1963 you're a rainbow of office girls,
sloshed on Coke Floats, a floriferous border, a Royal Park –
cute as a homegrown radish tucked in a pocket for later.

You are my layer-cake of sorbet, pink as kissed-off lipstick
and rose-petal jam. You are old with an iced croissant of hair
and you are young with custard candyfloss hair. Let's

watch the sun through glass the sun through boiled-sweet glass
the peeled sun through a cooked coach window the sun you keep
in your knees the way you can see something to make your heart wobble

and stash it for keeps. You try out the latest ultra-violet thoughts
as a skipping girl might not even consider on her first visit to the seaside
where are the clouds today but might think *I cannot possibly choose*

which pebble to keep. I really saw you today. Let me try on
your sunglasses. On me (!), but oh on you!

Your Year In Review

There was real snow. The little white record player
played Grandma's records. Your hair was Narnian and people
said you'd lost weight. You couldn't decide how shrill was too shrill.

Soup was austere, robust and recipes were exchanged.
Mould slunk along the windowsill, but you cleaned it off,
it's likely no one would have known. Insomnia made demands

January through March. Your heart went rogue. Desire,
kept in a gold compact, fell loose of its casing. Powder
went everywhere. Your hair and skirts got shorter. Some days

you were implacably indoors. As you gestured X close
all Y could do was recede. Z remained constant.
Life had an uneasy sheen, like butter

dropped on hot water. Someone you hoped a friend
looked in your eyes, smug as a zipped-up boot. The feeling
was wretchedly foreseen. Others leant in, but you skirted

their kindness. Late night buses became mirrors
you watched yourself crying in. You used up four
eyeliner pens and your three LBDs became five.

Holidaying in Turkey, you fooled over
a wastrel love and couldn't write a line. Saltwater,
molasses, boutique cats. You swam lengths

in the pool as though someone would keep count.
Money always a problem. Your act was not handsomely
together, still , there were pennies in the arcade for you.

There was too temporary a view of the sea. But
your first view of your nephew was his very first breath.
He was underwater too.

Little Elsie learned your name. Daily, the Sarahs
checked in and said all the right things. By autumn
the air was candied. You forced it. Invitations

came in. The kitchen dresser acquired a quirk
of glasses for sherry, Babycham and port. Invitations
went out, wine a necessary glaze.

Your year finds you alone. Recognise this person – friend.
Let go another – incident. Tilt up your chin. Pebbles
will always make the sound pebbles make when you walk on them.

"Too Gruesome!"

Rather a cupboard full of cut-off ponytails than this. I want a life
that allows excessive exclamation. Is not my bed a good bed?
Are my cupboards not stocked in the manner of someone who knows
    things?
Don't smirk. We're talking about me!

I need someone I don't know for the purposes of affirmation.
It may be Delores. We're in Palma, dining near the Cathedral.
We take to each other. She invites us to join her in Madrid. We each
have a cute gesture for 'airplane'. Delores has "an affinity with artists".
I knew you were a poet she says, gravely.
Most people in Palma dress drab, but Delores knows what suits her.
As we said goodbye, I took off the bracelet she admired and gave it to her.
She wept. Faux-wept. Wept.

R's convinced my problems are down to being a little 'too' most things.
Other friends marshal a rebuttal. Presently, I am creating a mind map
of cause and effect. Would you care to see my mood board (bedroom)?

      I imagine walking down the aisle to 'Clair de Lune' in primrose
          shantung silk.
      I dream in an Orenburg shawl.
      I imagine serenades. Look! The squirrels are skipping!
      I imagine my terribly sad divorce.
      I listen for ardent whispers, "never seen two people more in love".

C and I gloss our common woes. She takes that sofa and I take this.
In New York, she was described as a 'Smurf Angel'. In France
as 'Sapin de Noël', although faux-misheard as 'Lapin'. Everyone agrees
she is a Christmas Rabbit. Sometimes I buy makeup just to impress her.
When amores are badly behaved we chorus "Vintage Dino!"
and make our best faces-not-for-an-amore. We go together
but don't have compatible tastes in the roast potato department.

I wish ironed pillowcases counted for something,
though I've learned kindnesses don't. For a while there
I believed I could imbue affection by means of foot worship.
Silly ideas in that pretty little head! When asked a grand question
like 'What makes you happy?' I worry I'm answering from the point
of view of the me on a balcony in Majorca, drunk and rearing
a broken heart, my foot levitated to block out the moon.

I sign off with 'mille tendresse' and neutralise my self-image.

On My Deathbed, I Ask You This

Help me into fresh pyjamas,
lay out a blush-warm eiderdown
on a meadowed lawn, and grant me
a last lie-down in the edible air.

Preserve me that way – on a garden's feather
bed – my slunk body embroidered
with cobwebs, leaf drift, silver trails. Honour
this last voluptuous reluctance to leave.

Notes

The Scott and Zelda poems are corresponding collages of words taken from specific chapters of *Save me the Waltz* by Zelda Fitzgerald and *Tender is the Night* by F Scott Fitzgerald.